The Money Pie: A Recipe for Women Investors

The Philanthropy Pie: A Recipe for Leaving A Legacy

The Income Pie: A Recipe for Retiree

The Income Pie

A Recipe for Retirees

Carmen Portnoy

THE INCOME PIE

A RECIPE FOR RETIREES

A Blue Illumination Press Book / July 2026

ISBN: 978-1-962015-14-1

CONTENTS

FORWARD

Close your eyes. Take a deep breath. Imagine that in front of you is a delicious chocolate cream pie with a meringue topping.

No. Don't open your eyes.

Just smile as you see a dessert plate in front of the pie, a serving knife, and your fork. You are really going to enjoy that sweet and creamy chocolate goodness with a caramelized flavor from the meringue on top.

Be proud! You did it! This allegorical pie is made of money that you saved for many years in order to enjoy your retirement.

The tin represents your home. It gives you safety and shelter. But though it may appreciate in value over time, unless you sell, the walls will not feed you.

The crust of the pie is your cash. It keeps the rest of the pie stable. Cash will never fall in value. However, some years it will be thick and delicious, when interest rates are high, and sometimes very thin and dry, when interest rates are low.

The cream filling are your bonds. Unless you sell them, when they mature, you will receive your principal back and, in the meantime, the interest rate is fixed, so that you can count on that steady income to literally feed you.

And the top is a luscious meringue made of stocks, filled with air bubbles. It can tower when the stock market oven is running hot, but during a crash, can rapidly flatten.

The fancy name for the way this pie is combined is called Modern Portfolio Theory. It is a way of not just maximizing your return but also focusing on reducing risk, such as the 60/40 rule. You have 60% in stocks, which can provide a maximum return, with 40% in bonds. You don't earn as much in bonds, but they don't fall as much as stocks, historically.

You need to determine how much risk, or what your risk tolerance is, and by combining these different asset classes, you can achieve a more stable return. Are you comfortable if your savings fell by 50%? That is what happened to an all-stock portfolio in 2000-2002 and 2007-2008.

When I was younger, I focused on growing that meringue of stocks, but when I turned 55 and retirement became closer to reality, I started to become nervous.

The stock market had been up for 9 years, and I knew that I couldn't afford to retire into a bear market.

As a reminder, a bear fights by pushing down with its paws, and that represents the stock market falling and a bull fights by tossing its horns to the sky, which is when the stock market is going up.

I am fully retired now, and I have dramatically reduced my exposure to stocks for now.

The stock market is up over 400% since 2009. There was a long way to go to recover from the 2007-2008 bubble bursting. Interest rates are high. 10 tech stocks account for over 35% of the value of the S&P 500 Index as of April of 2026.

When you buy an index fund, and a common one is the S&P 500, one would assume that this is a diversified investment, since you are a shareholder in 500 companies, but unfortunately, that is not the case. The index is market weighted, which means the most expensive and overvalued stocks become a larger part of the overall investment, now dominated by tech stocks, such as Nvidia, Apple, Alphabet, Microsoft, Amazon, Meta and Tesla.

Now I have been wrong for the last 3 1/2 years. And yet, I would not hesitate to lighten my exposure to stocks again, since none of us can predict the future.

Why become so conservative?

Because I am retired now. If you enter retirement during a bear market, when you need to start withdrawing money to live, as an example, using 4% of your savings each year, in order to compliment Social Security and other investments you may have, if you have 80% in stocks, most projections are that you could run out of money in ten years.

If you are 30, 40 or 50 years old, you have time to add to stocks when they fall in value through dollar cost averaging, especially if you have a 401(K) where you are automatically buying into the stock market through good times and bad. You have time to recover.

But in retirement, we are no longer adding, we are withdrawing. We are reversing this process, spending down instead of building up.

If you don't want to ever work again, that money needs to be there to feed you and your loved ones, as medical expenses, vacations, food and even our streaming services keep going up.

Yikes! I haven't even started on how half our money pie can be plundered by inflation and taxes.

My focus has changed. Even though I saved for thirty years, in some ways I feel like I just blinked. Actually, I feel like I was stuffed in a circus cannon and was shot out through the air and landed 30 years later.

I have white hair. Severe arthritis in both hips. I have entered the youth of my old age. I've switched worrying about coloring my hair to being grateful I am still alive. My girlfriends and I don't talk about the cute boys we once dated. Now we discuss who our favorite orthopedic surgeon is.

But the fabulous news is that summer vacation is all year-round!

For the first year of retirement, I woke up every morning with a big smile on my face and said to my husband,

"Guess what?"

"You don't have to work anymore?"

"Yep!"

I no longer drive 20,000 miles a year to visit clients. I'm not in a St. John suit wearing bling and full war paint at 6:15 in the morning as I start my 45-minute morning commute to my big office with a glorious ocean view. I was always too busy to walk down to the sand for a visit.

I have not met one person who says they have regretted retiring. Surveys prove this.

We are happy as children and our happiness begins to decrease as all of our life demands increase. College, a career, marriage, children. All very satisfying and all a lot of work.

In retirement, many studies show that our happiness increases again, sometimes as high or even higher than in childhood.

So, I wanted to write this book to give advice to myself as well as to you, dear reader, on how to bake an Income Pie in a way to lessen financial worries, which can definitely get in the way of having fun!

In the following chapters, I will not only focus on the different sources of retirement income and the best ways to take them, but also on budgeting. It's a comfort to know that you have an allowance to spend and to enjoy. You worked hard and saved, and you earned it.

Here are different sources of income to cover your retirement expenses.

1. Social Security and Pensions.
2. Dividends from stocks.
3. Interest from cash, money market funds and CDs.
4. Bonds.
5. Annuities.
6. IRAs.
7. Rental Real Estate.

I will break them up into mini chapters.

Chapter 1

SOCIAL SECURITY AND PENSIONS

I will only devote a few paragraphs to pensions, since they are so rare these days.

If you have one, boy are you lucky!

To have a pension of 2K per month, (K) stands for $1 thousand dollars, you would have needed to save an additional 500K while you were working. For an example, over a 20-year career, that would be saving an extra 25K per year, assuming you did not have any appreciation. And appreciation cannot be assumed. There are plenty of people who saved diligently in their 401(K)s with too much exposure to stock mutual funds and had a huge crash right before retirement.

With a pension, the risk is with the company. One big issue that I saw throughout my career, though, was the choice one must make on the payout of the pension.

If you choose a pension payout based on your life, you receive the maximum amount each month. If you choose 75% for your life and 75% for your spouse's life, you will receive less on a monthly basis, but statistically, since the payout is based on two lives, not just one, the amount received will be greater.

One of you will live longer. Don't play Russian roulette and leave your spouse with zero. I have seen it happen. So ugly. We all have the same life expectancy if we get run over by a bus. Take a little less in order to receive the maximum total amount on both your lives and protect the both of you.

So, thank goodness for Social Security. When the Social Security Act was signed by Franklin D. Roosevelt in 1935, age 65 was set as the retirement age. Why? Because the average life expectancy at that time was also 65. We were not meant to receive payments for very long.

But through medical science, we learned about having a good diet, exercising, not smoking and the importance of community, as well as the discovery of great vaccines and antibiotics.

Our average life expectancy in 2026 in the United States is 77 for a man and 82 for a woman, if we don't take care of ourselves.

Well-educated people, and often, but not always, wealthier people, who eat lots of fruits, whole grains and veggies and walk a lot, maybe even swim or use a personal trainer or go to the gym regularly, have an average life span of 87 for a man and 92 for a woman in the U.S.

Yikes! How are we going to afford living so long?

Well, Social Security income helps. SSI for short.

Magazine articles and certainly the SS website, encourage us to wait. Wait until full retirement age. Even better, wait until you are 70. You will receive more. It will compound on average by 7%.

So why do the majority of Americans take their Social Security at 62? Are we all stupid?

No. Most of us need it early, due to health reasons or being laid off early because of ageism. We are not working due to physical reasons or simply that no one wants to hire us.

Or did you start to get really tired of working? Physically and mentally, ready for a permanent break?

I don't know about you, but once I reached 60, I had neither the patience nor the band width nor the strength in my lower back to sit in a car to commute, than sit in a chair all day working like a mad woman.

This is advice for the person who is no longer working. Take your SSI as early as you can. If you are still working, you will be heavily penalized for making over approximately 15K per year until you reach full retirement age. In my case that is 67.

Here is a secret. Statistically, we all receive the same amount of money. Some take it at 62 and live to 70. Some take it at 70 and live to be 100. Some take it at 70 and die at age 75. The actuaries at the Social Security Administration know it does not matter because—drum roll—yes, you know it is coming—

We don't know how long we will live and don't know if we will be in good enough health to enjoy it!

My advice? Take it as early as you can if you are fully retired, because you can always figure out a way to use it.

Travel? Yes, please. If you take SSI at 62, chances are you are still fairly spry, but as we approach 72, perhaps we will have more aches and pains, and by 82, maybe travelling is just a hassle.

The go-go years are from 62 to 72. The slow-go years are from 72 to 82. The no-go years are 82 plus.

Now your break-even point is 80 years old. That is when you will start to receive more income from your SSI payments because you waited until 70 to take your SS income as opposed to taking it early at 62.

No magazine article ever mentions the money you did not receive during that 8-year period.

As an example. You could receive 2K per month or 24K per year at age 62.

All the articles say *stop*. Wait. At 70 you could get 3K per month or 36K per year. So much more.

O.K. You wait. You receive zero for 8 years. You could have received 24K per year from age 62 to 70. That is $192,000 you did not get to spend.

So yes, in theory, 36K per year is more, but not if you consider that you did not get to spend 192K while you waited. That is your break-even point.

If you know you will live to be 100, then you will be the smartest kid on the block...when you are 80. But what if you were in a car accident and passed away at 71 and since you waited, you only received your SSI for one year?

But at 62, what about the enjoyment the extra 24K provided in those 8 years where you could still walk without pain in your knees and your hips? Priceless!

Now there are the rock stars among us who are in perfect condition and don't know why I am talking about aches and pains. God bless you for being perfect. I, however, look in the mirror each morning and am very surprised to see an old lady with white hair and wrinkles staring back at me. And I recall what Dianne Keaton said to a journalist.

“Now that you are aging, what do you consider is your best feature?”

“My eyes. I can look out and see how beautiful the world is.”

The time for vanity is over and the time for enjoying how beautiful life is in retirement has begun.

Chapter 2

DIVIDENDS FROM STOCKS

Stocks, sharing part-ownership in a company in the form of stock shares, are great when you buy low. It can hurt so bad, though, when you buy a speculative stock at a high and it drops 50% or more over a few weeks and never recovers.

As investors, we are formed by when we first start investing in stocks.

Most depression era people never invested in stocks after the 1929 crash. Only bonds and CDs and real estate. Who can blame them?

Those that started investing in 1990 had 10 incredible years, especially with investments in tech and growth stocks.

So that even after 3 years of bear markets, 2000-2002, where the total loss from peak to bottom was 50%, one could still be left with substantial gains if one did not sell.

Those of us who started investing in 1999 in internet stocks lost 90% of our investments. Once you are down that much, you never crawl your way back to a profit.

So 2000-2002 of bear markets, then a few great years of gains, and *wham*!

2007-2008. The real estate bubble burst. Took the stock market down for the ride. Caused the Great Recession. Yikes!

It took investors who started investing in stocks in 2007 ten years just to break even...assuming they held on and did not sell.

And now it is 2026. 16 years since our last recession. Colossal gains in stocks. Enormous gains in real estate. Cryptocurrency. Artificial Intelligence. Gold. Private Equity. Private Credit. Nvidia. Party on!

Let's ignore high inflation, insane tariffs, a huge deficit, increasing unemployment, struggling lower and middle-class Americans.

Someone who was 40 years old when they started investing in stocks in 2009 has had nothing but gains for 16 years. OK, a blip during Covid, where the market was down over 30% for one month, and a negative market in 2022. Now, back to new highs.

Everyone is dining on the sizzle, not the steak. There is rarely a mention of something as antediluvian as a P/E ratio. That is the price of a stock share divided into the earnings of the company.

Investing 101, as a reminder.

You become part owner of a company when you buy a stock share. A share in the profits, or losses of that company.

Traditionally, one would be willing to pay 10 to 15 times the future earnings of the company. And companies would try to grow at around 7% and then pay you a dividend of 3%.

That is what the average 10% compounding of stocks was based on. The current share price divided into the future earnings.

The stock market is considered under valued at 10 to 12 times earnings, fully valued at 15 times earnings and as of April of 2026, trading at 30 times earnings. Investors are paying twice as much as normal to own stocks.

If a company, let's call it X, does well, you receive two things. One is the price appreciation.

You paid $10 a share for X and now it is $20 a share.

Also, you receive part of the profits of the company paid back to you quarterly in the form of a cash dividend, if the company pays them.

Conservative investors like dividends. It is tangible proof that at least for now, this company is making real profits and sending us a thank you for being a partner in the company.

The dividend is paid quarterly, and it is based on the number of shares you own.

3 reminders:

1. They can stop paying the dividends at any time or lower it if they are struggling.
2. The company can go bankrupt and you can lose your entire investment.
3. Stocks have no safety net. They are not guaranteed. You can lose some or all of your investment.

I am in favor of dividend paying stocks, because while I want appreciation of the investments to grow over time, to keep up with or surpass inflation, I also want the 2%

to 3% dividend to be deposited into my checking account to help fund my retirement.

I use a wealth management advisor who guides me while investing with separately managed accounts. These are like mutual funds, but unlike a mutual fund, where my money is comingled with everyone else's, I own shares of each stock outright, with my own cost basis.

Using Charles Schwab or Vanguard are very popular ways to buy mutual funds on your own.

But do you change your own oil? Yes, perhaps, and congratulations.

But if you needed open-heart surgery, would you attempt to do it yourself? No, of course not. Your health is too important for that.

But your retirement savings? How important is it to keep your investments protected so you don't run out of your savings in the first 10 years of your retirement?

There are plenty of hypothetical calculations set on historical stock results based on the S&P 500 index that show a high probability of you running out of money after the first ten years of retirement if you start withdrawing 4% per year and start doing that while entering a bear market, with a portfolio overloaded with stocks.

Remember, from 2000 to 2002, we had a bear market that lasted for 3 years, and in 2007 to 2008, two years, and both times had an over 50% drop.

It's hard to wait for the stock market to recover when you are also withdrawing money at 4% to help fund your retirement. Many people at the bottom of previous bear markets sold their stocks and then found it difficult to find an optimum time to reenter.

If you are 30 and have 30 years to go, or you are 40 or 50, it does not matter. You can start investing today, perhaps at a stock market high, and enter a bear market, or you can reverse the scenario. You are saving and buying while stocks are cheap or doing the reverse. Time is on your side.

You are not taking money out, but adding to your 401(K) hopefully, during expensive and inexpensive periods.

Your outlook can change at 62. For me it did.

So back to dividends and an example.

I invest 100K with a dividend paying stock money manager, who focuses on well established companies that pay out part of their profit with an average of a 3% dividend.

I receive $3,000 a year, which is paid quarterly, $750 four times a year.

If these stocks fall to $50,000 and still pay the dividends, I will still receive $750 per quarter. If the investment doubles from 100K to 200K, I still receive $3,000 a year in dividends, since they are based on the number of shares that I own, not whether those shares went up or down in value.

Sounds great. Just remember, dividend paying stocks are still stocks. They are not guaranteed and they can lower or cancel the dividend payment.

That's why I am willing to pay ½% in a total fee to my financial advisor and to the money manager. I am not an expert at picking individual stocks. Frankly, I believe not many of us are. That is why that 100K portfolio is divided up between 30 to 40 different companies. Even an expert money manager realizes there is no way to predict future performance. Past performance does not indicate future results. But with a lot of research, 10 companies should do better than expected and account for the majority of the appreciation and 20 do around what was expected and 10 lose money and may have to be replaced.

I am charged a fee, not a commission, so the only incentive is to have my investments increase in value. That is the only way they get a raise.

I don't look for the cheapest investment, like a S&P 500 index fund. That's because it is market weighted. Instead of owning all 500 companies, you own the most expensive. Right now, the S&P 500 is a massive tech index, because the top ten holdings are all tech. I don't like that lack of diversity. Also, if you invest on your own, you may panic and sell at a stock market bottom. Then you wait to get back in, which is very difficult.

CASH IS KING

Chapter 3

CASH, CDS AND MONEY MARKET FUNDS

I love the old-fashioned expression, Cash is King.

I picture a king-sized bed made with soft cushy cash, to provide a safe and comfortable retirement income.

The best thing is that the price of the bed will never go down in value. In fact, if one makes sure not to have over 100K to 250K in any one bank, the FDIC, Federal Deposit Insurance Company, will step in to make you whole if the bank goes under.

The safe part is covered. However, the comfortable part is not. Just like stocks that fluctuate in value, the interest on your cash and CDs, (short term loans to a bank) is not.

It will go up and down according to the dictates of the Federal Reserve.

The Federal Reserve controls our economy. That is why the head of the Fed speaks in a dry and boring tone that could put a sheep to sleep.

Financial Advisors and institutional money managers know how powerful the Fed is, as well as economists and everyone involved in the financial markets.

The media and financial news? Not so much.

The Federal Reserve, or the Fed for short, hikes interest rates to slow the economy when the economy is growing too fast, because the death knell to consumers is high inflation. It is hard to get rid of.

So, when we become pleased because our cash is earning, for an example, 5%, it really is a danger signal that the economy could be running on fumes. About to croak.

A fancy word? A recession. A slow-down. A soft landing.

Note: We have never had a soft landing…ever.

Why? Because capitalism is based on issuing stocks and bonds and borrowing money to raise capital to expand. When it is cheap to borrow, companies, and especially real estate companies do so.

We buy homes. We borrow to purchase cars. It is easy to get credit cards and very easy to max them out. Companies feel flush with all that borrowed money and they do a lot of expanding and hiring. We watch as our share prices in these companies increase, sometimes rapidly, and we become greedy.

But when interest rates are at zero or 1%, for people who are in retirement, that is a body blow to our cash cushion.

100K in a cash money market fund was earning 5% in 2024. Now it is earning 3 1/2%. If we have a recession and the Fed cuts interest rates to 1%, our principal will not fall, but we lost 80% of our income from the high in 2024.

What helps create growth and spurs the economy does the opposite to our income flow invested in cash, CDs and money market funds.

The principal is safe. The income fluctuates based on the Fed. Their job is to keep inflation low and have stable employment. They are not considered with our income needs in retirement. They raise rates to slow down the economy when it overheats and inflation becomes too high. The economy is like a moving train and each interest rate hike is like a speed bump, until the huge train hits enough bumps and grinds to a halt, because we, as passengers on this train, panic. We stop buying because we are afraid and perhaps the higher interest rates on our credit cards and car loans are taking too much of a toll to handle. Companies begin layoffs. We suffer because we have lost our jobs. How can we make our super high mortgage payment, if we stretched and overpaid for our home? We default. We sell our stocks because we are terrified or we are forced to because we took on too much debt. Or something comes from left field that we could not predict. In 2002, the stock market might have been positive had that sad day of September 11, 2001 never occurred. Who knew we would be attacked? Who knew we would have had a pandemic in 2019 and the whole world would shut down?

It is prudent to keep a 6-month cushion of what you earn annually liquid for emergencies, if you can. If you live off 100K, keep 50K in cash. And of course, to pay for anything major within a year. A trip. A car. Helping with college tuition.

So here we are, April 2026. 16 years of wild appreciation in the stock market and real estate. The financial media estimating that yes, if the economy slows down, we may see a 10% drop in the value of our stock investments until they rise again. Perhaps the Fed will lower interest rates again. That will hopefully encourage more growth.

But a bear market is a mean and dangerous beast. It is wild. What starts off the rage is usually something that catches us by surprise. Maybe some crazy leveraged investments that erupt and create a panic.

One of the ways of investing that started off the Great Depression was that one could invest 10 cents and borrow a dollar. 90% leverage. That is why brokerage firms only allow you to borrow 50% against your stock portfolio. It is called margin borrowing. If your stock assets drop to below that minimum, you receive a "margin call", and you have only one day to raise cash to cover what you have borrowed. Now there are ways to borrow up to 300% against a mutual stock fund. They are called leveraged funds. So not 90% like in the 1920s or 50% now, but 300%. Sigh.

Cryptocurrency? Leveraged cryptocurrency? Gambling from individuals who act like investing is the same as going to Las Vegas? Investments that doubled in one year? In one month? In one day? I will discuss cryptocurrency, leverage, and other alternative investments in more detail in chapter 8.

30% of new investment accounts are being opened by teen-agers and people in their twenties. Young people have never experienced a bear market. When there is talk of “blood in the streets”, the look on their faces says it all.

"OK, Boomer".

Bears are big and mean and when they fight, those huge claws are out, pressing down, with foam in their mouths filled with gigantic sharp teeth.

A bear market is the stock market going down 25% or more, for more than six months. It is when there is a mass exit to sell crazy investments with insane profits—all on the same day. Get in line. Oh, your on-line brokerage firm can't answer your call, and the website crashed because everyone is trying to sell? It is so cheap to trade, so much fun, so easy. Until it is not.

People hate losing money twice as much as they like making money, once this hard lesson has been learned.

That is why if you plan to enter retirement with 80% to 90% of your investments in stocks, you could run out of money in ten years, if not sooner, because not only are your investments down, but you are compounding that by taking money out to live on.

I am more conservative than I have ever been. I don't understand the S&P 500 trading at 30 times earnings. Cryptocurrency is taking real money to buy fake money. Gold is only used for pretty jewelry. Why has it almost doubled in the last two years? Real Estate? A purchase price on a home for 2 million dollars, when Zillow can show anyone that you paid $800,000 for it five years ago? Do you have a buyer? The correct price for that home is what someone will write you a check for.

So even though I have been wrong since 2020, which is when I thought these insane prices could not keep rising, I am willing to be patient. I can't predict the future. But I can wait for it.

If there is a wallop of a recession, the Fed will lower interest rates rapidly, probably down to almost zero again.

The interest on your cash, CDs and money market funds will drop, because your bank is buying Treasuries from the Federal reserve at this suddenly lower interest.

So, this cash, this safe crust of your money pie, keeps your principal safe but not your income. The next chapter will be about the filling of your pie, with a more stable income stream. Bonds.

Chapter 4

BONDS

Bonds come in various forms, but they are all loans you make to either your federal, state or local government, to a foreign government, or to a corporation.

Loaning money to the US treasury is the safest investment we can make because even though we don't want to focus on this fact, Uncle Sam can raise our taxes at any time, as has been proven since our country was founded. Have you ever tried arguing with the IRS? Good luck. You can buy a Treasury bill, that matures in less than 1 year. Or a Treasury note, maturing, which means your principal is returned to you, in 2 to 10 years, or a Treasury bond, a loan that matures anywhere from 10 to 30 years. T is the letter used for the US Treasury. A T-bill, T-note or T-bond.

The T-bill is what the Fed issues to lower or raise our short-term interest rates. Banks purchase them, and that's why our money market fund interest increases or decreases based on this rate.

It is considered the risk-free rate of return. All other investments are compared to the current rate on this T-bill maturing in less than one year.

Municipal bonds, loans to our state or local municipalities, are tax-free because they are used to build our roads, schools, parks and bridges, etc. The Federal government says thank you, since you are helping provide this essential fund-raising service, by not taxing your interest. If it is a state bond purchased within your own state, there is no state tax due either.

If your state or local municipality is in good financial shape, there are rating companies that will give it an A rating, giving you guidance that the investment has risk, but not a lot. As an example, you might receive 4% tax-free. If it is a B rated bond, perhaps used to finance an airport or stadium, it may pay a higher interest, but that is because they have to attract investors.

Corporate bonds are riskier, because they are loans you make to a corporation. Ford, for an example. Ford may issue a corporate bond and ask you for a loan because it does not dilute the amount of common stock that has been issued. But Ford could go bankrupt. It seems unlikely but car companies have gone under. You might get paid back your principal but there are no guarantees. Since you are not helping your state or local government, you are fully taxed on the income.

High-yield bonds, and what I consider the true name for them, junk-bonds, are loans you make to risky companies desperately needing money. Instead of tempting you with a 5% interest rate, like Ford, they may wave an 8% or 9% interest rate in front of you. But if the company goes bankrupt, you lose your entire principal. I don't think that is a fair return, a slightly higher income with a risk of a total loss.

Once you buy any bond, until it matures, it will fluctuate in value. Your income, though, will not. As an example, you buy a 100K Muni bond paying 4% tax free, and you will receive the principal back in ten years. If you needed to sell it after one year, and interest rates are

5%, no one will give you 100K. Maybe only 90K, because why should they lock in the lower interest rate of 4%. Or maybe interest rates in one year are 3%. You might get more than you paid. The safest bet is to wait until maturity or hire an expert to purchase on your behalf.

I will give you an example of having 60% in stocks and 40% in bonds can provide you with steady income, on a investment of 800K. Let's assume you already own 480K in stocks, because the return on investing new money in stocks right now is highly unpredictable. We will focus on just the 320k investment in bonds, because they are predictable.

You give up future appreciation in order to receive income.

320K in 4% tax-free managed municipal bonds will provide you with approximately $12K per year, (it is actually $12,800, but I am assuming you pay $800 in fees). That will give you a tax-free income of $1,000 a month. In 30 years, you will probably only have $320,000 of principal, or less, but you will have received $360,000 of income.

Many investors focus on the fact that bonds don't appreciate in value, but that is not their purpose. They are there to provide you with income you can count on. Of course, just like stocks, if you invest 320k, the principal will fluctuate, until the bonds mature. They could drop to $288K if the bond market suddenly falls 10%, if people are convinced bonds are terrible since they don't rise dramatically in value, and only stocks are the investment to have, but, if you do not sell your bonds, you will still receive your 1K per month.

Municipal bonds pay interest every six months, but you can request to receive 1K per month. You don't have to wait. A laddered bond portfolio will have different bonds paying the interest at different times of the year, so some may pay in January and July, some in February and August, etc.

I love our municipal bond investments because as the old adage says, they help me sleep at night, because even though I see the price of them fluctuating slightly every day, the income we count on in retirement stays the same.

IRA

Chapter 5

IRAS

Like many Americans, perhaps you saved money every month and put it into your employer's 401(K). When you retire, you can leave it with the company, or you can "roll it over" into an IRA account that you control. If it goes directly to a brokerage firm, called a 401(K) to IRA direct transfer, there are no taxes due.

There is also a lot of media attention on rolling over a part or all of your IRA into a Roth IRA, because when you take out distributions, they will be tax-free and you will never be required to take out distributions. However, you are taxed that current year on the rollover from the IRA into the Roth IRA, which can raise your tax bracket, and you need to wait 5 years to withdraw, or you pay a 10% penalty on any earnings.

To anyone approaching retirement, I think it is a terrible idea. You could lose anywhere from 10% to 50% of your principal in current taxes to order to have, after 5 years, an asset where you pay no income taxes on withdrawals. An asset that could be worth 50% less because of all the taxes you paid in converting it from an IRA to a Roth IRA.

Since you did save income taxes when you contributed to your 401(K), when you take withdrawals, you will pay current income tax on the portion taken out.

You can now wait until you are 73. That is when you will have to take income out, known as required minimum distributions, or your RMD. It is based on the value of your IRA and your life expectancy.

But if you need income now and retire, for an example, at 62 or 65, and are waiting until you are forced to take withdrawals at 73, pause for a moment.

Would an extra 4% withdrawn from the value of that IRA be helpful to you now? You may enjoy using that extra money now, instead of waiting until 73. Maybe using the proceeds for a fun trip? That trip is what matters, those memories. At 73, you might not enjoy travelling as much.

Don't play "regretsy", (internet slang for regretting the stuff you purchased on the website Etsy).

Yes, you will have to declare that IRA distribution as income, but you did receive a tax break when you saved the money, and it grew without any taxes being paid while you were saving it. And only the amount taken out is taxed. The principal continues to grow without you having to pay taxes on interest or capital gains.

Roth IRAs are popular now with younger investors who earn under $150 thousand if single or under $228 thousand if married. The investments grow tax-deferred and when you withdraw funds after 59 1/2 years old, the income is also tax-free. However, you do not get a current tax deduction now. So you pay, as an example, 30 cents on every $1 dollar earned in taxes, in order to receive a tax benefit later.

I am withdrawing income from my IRA now, because though I would love to live to 100, if I get pancreatic cancer tomorrow, I'm not going to curse fate. Yes, I will be horribly upset. However, a cousin was diagnosed with this cancer and gone in only five months. He did not deserve an early demise either.

Live now. Enjoy now. Spend now.

Chapter 6

ANNUITIES

The concept of annuities is ancient. In Rome, you could donate your home and or your savings to the Temple and they would allow you to live there and would feed you for life. That was over two thousand years ago. Or in return for a lump sum, you could by an annua, a contract that guaranteed you a fixed yearly payment for life. They have remained popular ever since.

The temples have been replaced by insurance companies. An annuity is a contract with an insurance company that is specifically designed for retirement purposes. You make a payment to them, and they agree to pay out an income stream or a lump-sum amount at a future date. Combined with Social Security, they help us feel more secure that we will have predicable income to help fund our retirement.

You can't access the money until you are over 59 1/2, because the IRS treats annuities as a form of retirement savings, and the interest earned is not taxed until you start taking the income. If you sell one and have appreciation, the proceeds on all profits are considered ordinary income, not capital gains.

There are 4 major types of annuities.

1. Immediate lump-sum annuity.

2. Fixed Income annuities.
3. Fixed Income Indexed annuities.
4. Variable annuities.

The first three can be sold by insurance agents, and so you will encounter a pitch on those first three much more often. A variable annuity requires, in addition to an insurance license, that the broker pass an SEI exam, a Series 6 or 7 exam, a Series 63 state security registration, and you must be affiliated with a FINRA-registered broker-dealer firm.

Also, the first two usually pay the insurance agent 2% to 4% and number 3, the Fixed Income Indexed annuity will pay them between 6% to 9%. If you want to cash out before the insurance company earns back this commission they paid out, you will have to pay it, using the fancy term called a surrender charge. The insurance salesperson can state that you will pay absolutely nothing to purchase this annuity, and that is correct. They are paid by the insurance company. But the surrender charge to leave the contract is what you will owe and the reason it is there is because no one works for free! Also, in terms of incentive, it would seem that an insurance broker would rather be paid 6% to 9%, instead of a lower amount. That is why you will most likely be approached to purchase one of these FIA's or Fixed Indexed Annuities. I will explain more the dangers of you seeing a substantial loss by purchasing an FIA, but first, let's go over the first two.

1. In an immediate lump-sum annuity, as an example, if you invest 100K, the life insurance company may pay you 5K annually or 5% for life, or 6K or 6% if you are 70 years old or even 8K or 8% if you are age 80 years old.

The payment will be higher at 80, because they expect you will pass away sooner, and part of the income you receive is your principal being returned to you. They keep whatever principal is left when you are gone. If you are married and it is based on both your lives, the interest offered will be less. If you live to 100, then you could even receive more in income that the initial investment. They hope you will have a short life expectancy, since they will keep more of the lump-sum of your investment. So, this is not an investment for funds you want to leave to your heirs.

2. A fixed annuity is like purchasing a bond, but you are entering a contract with an insurance company. They may offer you 5% for ten years, and it will grow tax-deferred until you start taking income. I would suggest buying a municipal bond instead. The interest also on a Muni bond will not be taxed if purchased in your state, and there is much more flexibility, because you can sell the bond at any time, even though you may receive less than you paid for it if you sell it before it matures. The income, though, is stable. Once again, a fixed annuity will have a surrender charge, which you will have to pay in order to terminate the contract.

3. The FIA or fixed indexed annuity, which pays the insurance salesperson the most, is also the most dangerous, where you could have a substantial loss.

Let me explain why. You are offered this great investment, where it protects you if there is stock market decline, but you can participate in the market rising and may even receive a higher income stream. Sounds great! However, usually the downside protection is only 10% to 15%. If the stock market index falls 50%, which it has done twice, both in 2000-2002 and 2007-2008, you will not go down 50%, which is wonderful, but you will go down 40%, if you have a 10% downside protection.

But the worst thing about these investments is that they cap your upside. So perhaps the maximum upside you can receive would be 15%.

This is complicated, so here is an example.

If you invest 1 million in a FIA, and the stock market index it is linked to falls 50%, your contact value will be now $600K. But you need to go back up 66% to just break even.

How can that happen when your upside is capped at 15%?

That means if you invest in one of these at the height of the S&P 500, your $1 million could drop to $600 thousand, and then up another 15% gain that was capped would mean you have locked in that loss, because your contact is now worth only $690 thousand with an upside of 15%.

Here is an official warning that I pulled from a major brokerage firm website. "Owners could see a substantial loss during an index period if the index declines more than the level of downside protection. If the owner does see a substantial loss during an index period, the owner may not be able to participate fully in a subsequent market recovery due to the capped upside potential in subsequent index periods.

In plain terms, I would highly recommend you *not* purchase one of these!

4. A variable annuity can come in many shapes and sizes, but essentially you will have your investment, as an example, 100K, put into 2 buckets. One will vary, or

fluctuate in value, hence the variable in the annuity name. It will be in a group of mutual funds, usually with the maximum of 60% to 70% in stock funds. The other bucket, which is insured by the insurance company, will state, as an example, that no matter what that initial 100K investment fluctuates by, you will receive at least a guaranteed 4% income to be used to help fund your retirement. And most of them also state that if the variable bucket of mutual funds has more than a 4% appreciation, on the initial date that you invested your 100K, let's say on March 23, that on each March 23 going forward, they will adjust the growth of the 4% income and step-up the contract using the variable amount.

Wow, sounds complicated? Well, yes it is. So here is an example. Imagine that on March 23 of 2020, you invested 100K in a variable annuity with a 4% guaranteed minimum income. It was 5 years before you decided to retire. It just so happened to be at the very bottom of the pandemic stock market selloff that only lasted for one month.

Your investment in the bucket containing stock and bond mutual funds has now doubled in value, since it continued to grow each year, and that value was captured on March 23 of every year since then. The 4% minimum guarantee you will now receive will be based on 200K. And if we have a stock market crash and you see that variable value drop to 125K, the insured value will remain at 200K.

So instead of getting 4k a year when you start taking income, you will receive 8k a year, and that will never go down, even if the value of the stock and bond bucket drops to zero. Your insurance contract states that you will have the chance to annuitize, i.e., enter into a bet with the insurance company on how long you will live, and they will have to provide you with that 8K for life. Once again though, once you do annuitize, the principal that is left over will remain with the insurance company.

And please remember how expensive your home and health and car insurance is. They don't provide this for free. The annuity company can charge anywhere from 1% to 3% to insure your income on the stock and mutual fund bucket, as well as about a 1/2% fee annually to pay the mutual fund money managers. It won't ever come out of the 4% guaranteed income bucket, but these annuities are expensive, definitely.

There are variable annuities that charge no surrender fees, which means you can leave at any time. However, there will be another fee that is removed every year for a period of years from the stock and bond mutual fund bucket to pay the insurance or stockbroker or financial advisor who sold you the contract.

I always went over in great depth and length explaining the pros and cons of variable annuities, including all of the insurance fees and how I was paid. I preferred to receive compensation annually, usually over a four-year period, than receive 4% upfront, and not have the client pay a surrender charge if they changed their minds. That way I needed to earn their business over those four years. Never trust someone who says that they are not receiving compensation. We are not volunteers. We don't work for free.

Often people who have maxed out their 401(K)s and are risk adverse will save money in this type of annuity. Just like an IRA, if you need your principal or income before age 59 ½ you will pay a 10% penalty, because the investments will grow tax-deferred, like in your IRA or 401(K) until you begin taking withdrawals.

I have a portion of our investments in variable annuities, because I think paying for insurance on my retirement income is worth it, and I can take more risk than I normally would, with stock and bond mutual funds in the variable bucket. And I haven't paid any taxes or capital gains yet. When we start taking withdrawals, the monthly income amount will be taxed, but not the principal.

Some annuities are great. Many are horrible investments. All of them are complicated, because you are paying an insurance company to take the risk away from you losing your principal, and insurance is never cheap.

Don't buy one with surrender charges. A broker can receive a hefty commission for selling you one. You don't pay the commission. The insurance company pays it. However, they want you to stay as a client for as long as possible to justify the cost of paying the broker upfront.

Don't buy one if the broker can't show and explain to you in the contract exactly what are all the fees, commissions, and surrender charges.

And I would not recommend ever investing more than 25% of your principal in one. Easy to purchase and difficult to liquidate. You will need to transfer to a different annuity if you want all of your principal back, otherwise you will have to pay taxes on the appreciation you made. Remember the 100K example that grew to 200K? Uncle Sam is hungry and will take a big bite of that 100K of appreciation, all to be taxed as ordinary income unless you transfer it into another annuity. Better to consider this as a SS income supplement and only take the guaranteed income benefit.

Chapter 7

REAL ESTATE

Real estate is attractive to many investors because stocks and bonds are intangible. We can't reach out and touch them anymore, as they now exist only as numbers on our statements. With real estate, we can walk into a physical piece of property and touch the walls. We can buy little fixer-uppers and rent them out. Our homes provide us shelter and we don't have to sell if the price drops in value.

And over the long run, R.E. (Real Estate) appreciates by 5% a year on average.

It can be a great part of your retirement nest egg. Many people have done very well with real estate rental properties.

Any investment is good if you purchased it at a low price and it has appreciated in value. And it can be a poor investment if you have overpaid.

If you are a landowner, obviously you can have either good tenants or bad tenants. Sometimes it can be heart wrenching because a good tenant can have a sudden loss, their job or their health, and can't pay their rent.

It is a moral dilemma that stock and bonds don't have.

Do you give them a chance? Or does Shakespeare's phrase, "neither a borrower nor a lender be," come to mind.

Eviction is not easy. Neither is a terrible tenant who sues you over a non-existent insect or mold problem or simply trashes the place.

Property managers can help, if they are doing their job properly, but they don't work for free. And then there are property taxes, utilities, insurance, repairs, etc.

And many landlords don't add the work hours of their "free" labor when they calculate their profits after all of these expenses. And the end profit is taxed!

Is it concerning when Zillow shows a home that 6 years ago sold for 400K, and now someone just purchased it for 800K? At a normal growth rate of 5% per year, the property should be worth 536K. A 400K profit is 16% per year.

To qualify for an 800k mortgage, perhaps it took the earning power of a couple both earning fairly high salaries. What if one of them loses their job?

Condos are particularly difficult to keep up their value, if you overpaid, because HOA fees can increase at any time and you do not own the land, just the condo. That is why Condos fluctuate the most in price.

But if you don't mind the work involved in being a landlord and don't take on a lot of debt to buy rental property, and especially if you buy when R.E. is low, it can be a marvelous investment.

There are also REITs, Real Estate Investment trusts. They are sold on the premise that you are more diversified because the money managers can purchase large pieces of real estate because you have pooled your money with a group of other investors. But you don't own the real estate outright and if there is a drop in real estate prices your investment will also drop.

WALL ST
NEW YORK STOCK EXCHANGE

Chapter 8

A CONFESSION

OK, now is the time for the true confession of this retiree.

I started as a Financial Advisor in 1997. We had 3 up years before the 2000-2002 dot.com bubble burst.

The stock market was then in a bear market...for the next 3 years. We thought 2002 would be the recovery year, until 9/11/2001. So very sad and tragic and in the heart of the financial district and the Pentagon.

We had 4 up recovery years and then the great recession hit in 2007-2008.

And now I own municipal bonds and annuities, and I have way too much in cash. My stock exposure is a paltry 20%.

I was extremely worried about entering retirement, taking income from my investments, while experiencing another terrible bear market. If that were to happen, I could run out of money in ten years.

So, I retired. And I have been wrong since 2020.

The 2020 bear market, caused by the pandemic, lasted only one month.

The 2022 bear market was not only difficult for stocks but was the worst year for bonds—in history!

I am still waiting. My husband, and it seems, all the rest of investors in the US are convinced that a recession will not happen.

What? Ever?

I didn't understand the dot.com tech prices. I didn't understand the 2007-2008 bear market caused by crashing real estate prices.

I am writing this as of April 2026. 40% of the entire S&P 500 stock index is made up of ten tech companies. So many people are buying crypto currency and gold and private equity and private credit and real estate and stocks with the highest inflated values, ever.

I will give you an explanation of cryptocurrency, gold, private equity, private credit and AI.

Cryptocurrency is taking real money to buy fake money, using a system called block chain. You then store your fake money in a ledger, which is a computerized database. You need two keys, or very strong passwords, to access it. If you forget one of them, you lose your entire investment! 25% of all investors have done this. You may hear in the news that you can buy a home using cryptocurrency. This is false. Your bank will allow you 60 seconds to sell your cryptocurrency at its current price in order to receive real money, which then the bank takes in order to purchase your home. Any gains you may have are subject to capital gains tax. Warren Buffet calls cryptocurrency "rat poison squared."

Gold is shiny and used for jewelry. In 1971, President Nixon officially converted the US dollar into a fiat currency, no longer backed by gold. It is backed by the power to tax us. That is why the US currency, T-bills, T-notes and T-bonds are considered so safe. The government can raise our taxes at any time. It has been many years of our taxes being lowered, but we do have an enormous deficit because of this. All the gold ever mined would fit into 3 Olympic sized pools. It does not produce anything. It does not grow. It does not employ people. It does not provide income. Gold prices do not derive their value from an underlying business. The price is mainly driven by emotion and speculation. It is not a good hedge against inflation. It tends to go through long periods of underperformance followed by brief spikes. Which is where we are now.

Private equity are investments you can make privately, as opposed to buying stock in a public company on a registered exchange. Since it is private, all the reporting done is on a voluntary basis and also all the valuations too. It is opaque and you tie up your money for long periods of time. Usually if you want your money back, you are only allowed to receive 5% at a time. Supposedly, you should receive a higher rate of return, but honestly? How do you know? It may look great on paper but if you can't get your money back?

And you need to be an Accredited Investor in order to purchase into one of these, with an annual income of over $200 thousand if you are single and $300 thousand if you are married, or you need to have a net worth of over $1 million, not including the value of your home. So, the excuse for not enough public scrutiny and purchasing a non-liquid investment, if that you are supposed to be a "sophisticated investor" once you earn this amount per year, or have this amount saved. Oh really? I had plenty of doctors and lawyers and business owners who were brilliant at what they did but had not time or inclination to understand investments.

One thing they really did not like, in addition to all the secretive nature of these investments, was the 2 and 20 rule.

The firm charges you a minimum management fee of 2% and then once they achieve over a target return, for an example, of 8%, they get to keep 20% of the profits.

That is why hedge-fund managers are so rich! They try to have a breakout year and make a huge profit, and then they take 20% of the profits. The next year, they can close shop. And with voluntary reporting of returns, only the firms making a profit report. The other ones don't have to.

Private credit is much the same as private equity, but instead of investing in companies, they lend companies money. Why not just go to the bank? Because the companies they are lending money to are so risky that banks won't lend them money. Another name for them is "shadow banks." They have lent a lot of money to AI companies.

AI. Artificial Intelligence. Wow, computers that will do all of our thinking for us. Maybe that will be a good thing. Who knows? But right now, AI companies have stock prices that are incredibly overvalued, because they are not making a profit. If you make $100 million but spend $500 million, you have a $400 million loss. It costs an enormous amount of energy to calculate using these extremely rapid methods. So they need expensive chips and data centers. A large data center needs to be cooled, requiring enough water to service a town of 50 thousand people...every day. Plus electricity. There are now over 4,500 data centers across the US, using 4.4% of all of our electricity, enough to power 16 million homes. Of course, they are also used for streaming services, our business and home computers, but the huge build up is from the demands of AI.

My comfort, if you can call it that, is two sayings by Warren Buffet.

“Rule No. 1: Never lose money. Rule No. 2: Never forget Rule No. 1.”

And “What the wise do in the beginning, fools do in the end.”

Income I do understand, from bonds, cash, SSI, pensions, annuities and cash. And stock dividends, even though a company can decide to lower or eliminate them.

CAFÉ DE FLORE
CAFÉ
CROISSANT
VIN
FROMAC
PARIS

Chapter 9

FINDING IT HARD TO SPEND

Now that I have retired, I understand when my retired clients said they found it hard to spend money. Here are the steps I would go through with them.

1. I know what my income is from SSI, interest from my bonds, cash, dividends from stocks, and annuity income.
2. I have a budget.
3. I know what my fixed expenses are. Property taxes. Utilities. Insurance, car, health, and property. Cable. The Gardener. Cleaning service. Food.
4. I know on average how much we spend on extras like restaurants, streaming services, clothes, hair, nails, gym membership, and travel.
5. I know on average how much I give to charity.

But I'm afraid. Inflation scares me. Prices keep rising and I don't want to pay higher prices!

So, I tell myself what I told my clients. Take a zero off the end of the price. My husband hates this concept, this "girl" math. But it does not have to make logical sense, because we are dealing with our fears and our emotions.

No. I can't do this, buy this, give this, or travel there because it costs too much.

But I have a budget. My income vs my expenses.

Charles Dickens said that "a man who has one hundred pounds a year to live off, and spends one hundred pounds, will have a happy life. The man who has one hundred pounds and spends one hundred and ten pounds will end up in debtor's prison."

If you have an income of 100K and spend 100K, and you do not count on appreciation from stocks and real estate, which will fluctuate, but from your SSI and rental income, pension, interest from bonds, dividends from stocks, etc. and you know what your fixed expenses are, then spend the rest!

Your job and my job, too, in retirement is no longer to save but to spend. As long as you don't overspend and stay within your budget, you will be fine.

If your grocery bill comes to $80, take a zero off it, and make it $8! Yes, it is inflation, but your income inflated also.

Fifty years ago, your income in retirement could have been $10K. $8 paid for groceries is the same as $80 if your income is 100K per year.

Like I said, my husband go nuts and calls this fuzzy math. I call it the emotional stability I need not to go around freaking out about the high prices of everything. We worked hard and saved and had appreciation over the last thirty years on our assets in order to pay for these prices now.

Chapter 10

THE FINAL THIRD

I will now go over what we think as obvious cliches, but, dear reader, I need to hear them. I am not lecturing you, but myself.

We are in the home stretch of our lives. Travel now. Indulge now. Spend now. Enjoy now. Give now.

Create memories. If that business class ticket of $5000 is stopping you from traveling, use points for part of it and take a zero off the end. $500 is much more reasonable. Fuzzy math logic, but with my bad back and a 15-hour flight to Australia, I am sucking it up and paying that, with partial points, because it is in my travel budget.

Magical realism in retirement.

Who do you want to be in retirement?

How about a writer? So write. It is a physical process, like running a marathon. I write from 10 am to 2 pm Mondays through Fridays. Mainly romance novels because they are fun.

Buy a big paper calendar and a notebook. Write down what you want to do and who you want to be.

Connect to your community. Volunteer or join your local Rotary club. I have been a Rotarian since 1997. We meet each week, have excellent speakers from local non-profits, university presidents, directors of local theater groups. It is a great way to find out the wonderful, good work that volunteers are doing, in case you would like to get involved.

You don't have to join. Find your local club. Go for a month. Listen to speakers. Ask other people where they volunteer. You will easily find yourself as busy and productive as when you were working.

How much fun is it that our time is our own and we can do what we like? Gardening, taking a painting class, playing pickle ball with friends, hiking, having friends over for lunch or dinner.

How many of us at work had vision boards and/or brainstorming meetings and mission statements?

Did you ever have to compile a list of tasks you accomplished each week for your company?

Your company is now you!

I need to exercise to keep my building from crumbling.

So, when I retired, I wanted to return to swimming. I put on the paper calendar, swimming 2:30 to 3:30 PM on Tuesdays and Thursdays and 11 AM on Sundays.

Then I put Post-it notes on my computer and on the bathroom mirror and the fridge.

Swimming Tuesday at 2:30!

I didn't want to go swimming, but I had joined the YMCA, and I had already put all my swim gear in the trunk.

"Just go dip your toes in the water for ten minutes."

Afterwards, naturally, I felt great. And did laps for 15 minutes and built up from there.

And the Post-it note went up for Thursday and then Sunday. Until it became a habit.

"Put on your tennis shoes and walk for ten minutes. Go to the gym and just stretch for 15 minutes."

These are my internal instructions to motivate myself. And ten minutes turns into 30 minutes usually.

All we need is thirty minutes a day. When I was working, I was running between appointments, gathering reports, running to the copier machine. Fit bit wasn't a hit marketing item yet, but I was definitely getting in my steps.

Like a budget to know what your expenses are, make a time budget to see how you spend your hours.

I found myself in retirement reading four different newspapers in the morning, often for more than two hours. Now I am on a complete social media blackout and I try to limit my reading to the Wall St. Journal at 30 minutes.

Why? Because my bookshelves are full of classic British, Russian, French and American authors and I want to reread my favorites again.

Travel. Do you want to travel but your spouse does not? No problem. You know where to find them when you return. Call a friend and go with them. Do what you want to do.

When we were working, how much time did we have with our significant other anyway? Sometimes a little time away is what is needed.

I know my angel hubby loves me and I adore him, but sometimes I feel like a tattered door mat.

But when the cute chatter box (me) who makes the delicious food every evening is gone? The one I can easily ignore is now the South of France with a couple of her girlfriends?

I went on an incredible cruise with my best girlfriend, crossing the Atlantic from Miami to Rome. 16 days, with 10 days at sea.

My husband, when asked first, said,

"I would go insane trapped on a boat with ten days at sea and nothing to do."

What did my girlfriend and I do? Slept in late. Took Zumba classes. Ate delicious food. Went to the gym. Ate more yummy food. Went to the theater lounge 30 minutes before the 9:30 PM show to get great seats for the upcoming enthusiastic if cheesy entertainment. Saw every silly musical and comedy/magician act. Then we went dancing afterwards. We had such a great time!

I want to travel for six weeks each year. That's my retirement dream. My husband can handle 4 weeks, so I tack on an extra two weeks at the beginning or the end of the trip with a girlfriend or two.

It works. Marriage is through sickness and though health, but that doesn't mean you have to stay home all the time if your spouse is a homebody.

ROAD TO RETIREMENT

Epilogue

Throughout my long career as a Wealth Management Advisor and Certified Financial Planner, every client was radiant at our next meeting after their retirement. Not one said that they regretted their decision, except to ask,

"Why didn't I do this earlier?"

* * *

It's been fun, writing this Income Pie. It's advice I need for myself, as well as for you, dearest reader.

Enjoy, and thank you for the inspiration.

Made in the USA
Monee, IL
04 November 2026

67377403R00046